W9-BZM-215

OCT - - 2010

SUSTAINING OUR ENVIRONMENT

Water

Jill Laidlaw

amicus

Published by Amicus
P.O. Box 1329, Mankato, Minnesota 56002

Printed in the United States of America at Corporate Graphics, in North Mankato, Minnesota.

Published by arrangement with the Watts Publishing Group Ltd., London.

Library of Congress Cataloging-in-Publication Data
Laidlaw, Jill.
 Water / by Jill Laidlaw.
    p. cm. -- (Sustaining our environment)
 Includes index.
 ISBN 978-1-60753-140-1 (hardcover)
 1. Water--Environmental aspects. 2. Water use. 3. Water supply.
 4. Hydrological cycle. I. Title.
 GB662.3.L35 2011
 333.91--dc22

                        2009028258

Series editor: Adrian Cole
Art Director: Jonathan Hair
Design: Simon Borrough
Picture Research: Diana Morris

Acknowledgements:
AFP/Getty Images: 29r. Scott Barbour/Getty Images: 29t. Fethi Belaid/AFP/Getty Images: 2br. Kike
Calvo/VW Pics/Alamy: 13. David Chernitsky: 35. Christian Aid: 25l, 26. Dinodia: 21. Doga Yusuf
Dokdok/Shutterstock: 10. Image courtesy of Earth Sciences and Image Analysis Laboratory, NASA
Johnson Space Center: 20. Earthwatch: 32t. Robert Granfiore/Getty Images: 18. Getty Images: 31, 33.
Greenshoots Communications/Alamy: 11t. Tomas Havisham/Panos: front cover. Stephan
Holeman/istockphoto: 37. Fred Hoogervoorst/Panos: 30. Richard Jones/Sinopix/Rex Features: 39.
Tul Karem/Rex Features: 27bl. Dave Martin/Getty Images: 16. Indranil Mukerjee/AFP/Getty Images:
17. NASA: 14, 15bl. Dmitry Naumov/Shutterstock: 8. Robert Nickelsberg/Liaison/Getty Images: 34.
NOAA: 38t, 38b. Mike Page: 25r. Potters for Peace: 24. Visal Shah/Shutterstock: 22. Ana
Sousa/istockphoto: 9. Sven Torfinn/Panos: 40. DaDang Tu/Reuters: 36. Robert Wallis/Panos: 23, 28. ©
Water Corporation Western Australia/Darryl Peroni: 19. David Jay Zimmerman/Corbis: 41.

1213
32010

9 8 7 6 5 4 3 2 1

Contents

The Water of Life

Earth is known as the Blue Planet for a reason—71 percent of the world's surface is covered with water. Every living thing depends on water for life. It is difficult to imagine us running out of it, but some people think that is exactly what is happening. This book looks at the key environmental and social issues linked with water and highlights what is being done to try to make water sustainable for all.

Is Water Renewable?

Of all our natural resources, water should be the easiest one to sustain because the water cycle—the natural cycle where water evaporates, rises into the air, becomes part of a cloud, and then falls back to us as rain—continuously renews our water supply. But while it is renewable, is it sustainable? Why is water viewed as a current or potential environmental problem at all?

Thanks to rain, water is the ultimate renewable resource. The water cycle continuously replenishes our groundwater supplies, but we have to be careful not to extract groundwater more quickly than it can be replaced naturally. ▼

"If there is magic on this planet, it is in water."

Loren Eisley (1907–1977), American ecologist and poet

Measuring Water
- Cubic foot (ft³)—could fill about one side of a kitchen sink
- Cubic meter (m³)—could fill about three bathtubs
- Cubic mile (mi³)—could fill about 96,000 Olympic-sized swimming pools
- Cubic kilometer (km³)—could fill about 400,000 Olympic-sized swimming pools

What Is Sustainable Water?

A sustainable water supply is one that meets the continuous drinking, washing, sanitation, cooking, and consumer needs of all individuals—whether they are farmers or office workers—without impacting negatively on other human beings, on animals, plants, or on the environment—particularly water-based ecosystems such as wetlands, rivers, or oceans.

Is Water Sustainable for All?

Estimating the chances of water being sustainable depends on how much access to water people have, and how much of it they use. For example, a man living in the U.S. uses an average of 67,098 cubic feet (1,900 m^3) of water a year, whereas someone living in Gaza in the Middle East only has access to 11,300 cubic feet (320 m^3) of water a year.

Agricultural production also uses different amounts of water depending on where it is and the crop being grown. For example, farmers in Africa cannot produce the same amount of food every year because the rainfall changes from year to year, and state-provided water supplies can be unreliable and expensive. However, farmers in Spain can afford to import water from other countries to water their crops in drought-ridden years. Cotton, rice, and sugar are among the most thirsty crops, and need much more water to grow. Water highlights the inequalities between nations and individuals.

What Are the Right Questions?

So, perhaps we need to ask different questions if we want to find out more about sustainable water, such as: in the future, can water come to be seen as a global resource that needs to be distributed fairly? Can people learn to use water more efficiently than they currently do?

Most freshwater is stored in the polar ice caps as ice—and cannot easily be used by people for drinking, farming, or industry. ▼

Types of Water

- The oceans make up 97.2 percent of the world's water—but we cannot drink it because it is saltwater.

- Most freshwater (2.15 percent of the world's water) is locked up in the polar ice caps—so we cannot get to it—and even if we did, it would be environmentally damaging.

- Freshwater that we can drink makes up only 0.65 percent of all the water on Earth.

Water Wars?

There is only so much clean freshwater to go around. With the world's population rising rapidly, increasing food demands, and expanding industry, there is a very real danger that our water needs will outstrip supply. In many places this is already happening. Do we face a future where armies have to stand guard around rivers, lakes, and reservoirs? Will water become the most valuable commodity a nation has to trade? Some politicians and environmentalists think that water is the next oil—a precious resource that nations could be willing to go to war over.

The Nile River flows through ten nations in Africa, including Egypt. The Nile Basin Initiative was formed in 1999 to establish "the equitable utilization of, and benefit from, the common Nile Basin water resources."

Fighting for Water

So far, no large-scale wars have been fought exclusively over water as a resource—but numerous disputes and violent attacks have. This has happened between countries, between communities, and between individuals. So while rivers flow along their natural course, wherever you look in the world —from the Danube River in Europe to the Jordan River in the Middle East—access to and control of water is a major cause of boundary disputes, diplomatic tension, and armed conflict.

On July 20, 2006, Sri Lankan Tamil Tiger rebels in control of a sluice gate refused to open the gate, cutting off the water supply to 60,000 people and hundreds of rice fields in the government-controlled area nearby. The Tigers said they shut the gate because the government failed to keep its promise to build a reservoir in a rebel-held territory. The Sri Lankan government eventually responded with a military attack that killed six Tamil Tiger cadets. Seventeen aid workers from the French-based Action Against Hunger NGO were also killed, but responsibility for their deaths has not been established.

Israel and Palestine both tap underground aquifers for water, but Israel pumps more of this water than the Palestinian territory. This has led to the Palestinians accusing Israel of stealing their water.

> "It is no accident that the violence in Darfur erupted during the drought . . . When Darfur's land was rich, black farmers welcomed Arab herders and shared their water. With the drought, however, farmers fenced in their land to prevent overgrazing . . . For the first time in memory, there was no longer enough food and water for all."
>
> Ban Ki-Moon, Secretary General of the United Nations, March 2008

Case Study: Every River Has Its People

Projects such as Every River Has Its People (ERP) work to remove or mediate the tensions between nations caused by shared water resources.

In southwest Africa, Namibia, Angola, and Botswana all share the Okavango River Basin. Between 2004 and 2007, the ERP project used specially-designed posters and leaflets in local languages to inform the communities that depend on the Okavango River Basin of the strains that were being placed on this fragile ecosystem. The ERP gathered information and involved ordinary people in the decision-making process. The ERP asked local people what problems they were encountering, such as rival communities overfishing, and

then worked with them to find solutions and to develop a coordinated management plan for the whole Basin area. The next phase of the project will run until 2012, and focus on consulting people at both a community and a national level on the sustainable comanagement of the natural resources of the Okavango River Basin.

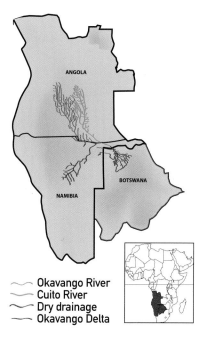

~ Okavango River
~ Cuito River
~ Dry drainage
~ Okavango Delta

▲ This map shows the rivers and major drainage networks that flow into the Okavango River Basin across three countries in Africa.

◀ In southwest Africa, water management projects have eased the way for cooperation over water resources between communities that have grown suspicious of each other.

Virtual Water Footprint

In order to manage our water resources we need to understand how much water we use. We all have a water footprint: the amount of water we each use every day. It is estimated that an average household in the U.S. uses about 100 gallons (379 L) of water a day to do things such as drinking, flushing the toilet, and watering the lawn–but we use about 30 times this amount (about 58 bathtubs of water) in the form of "virtual" water.

Virtual Water

Virtual water is the amount of freshwater that was used to produce the things we use. Here are some examples.

- There are 1.5 cups (.35 L) of water in a soft drink, but it takes 845 cups (200 L) of virtual water to grow and process the sugar in the drink.

- It takes 37 gallons (140 L) of virtual water to provide one cup of coffee.

- Someone who eats a meat-and dairy-based diet uses about 1,320 gallons (5,000 L) of virtual water a day, but a vegetarian only uses about 528 gallons (2,000 L).

- The tables on the left show the world's top six agricultural water importers, measured in Gm³ (billion cubic meters) per year. Of course, this is all freshwater.

List of top six net agricultural virtual water importers (Gm³/yr)

Country	Export	Import	Net import
Brazil	91	199	107
Mexico	19	103	84
Japan	4	86	83
China	55	133	78
Italy	38	88	50
UK	15	55	40

List of top six net agricultural virtual water exporters (Gm³/yr)

Country	Export	Import	Net import
USA	298	137	161
Australia	71	10	62
Argentina	58	4	54
Canada	70	27	44
Thailand	52	9	43
India	66	24	42

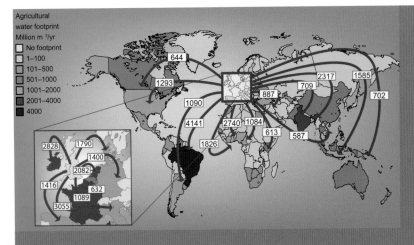

Agricultural water footprint
Million m ³/yr
- No footprint
- 1–100
- 101–500
- 501–1000
- 1001–2000
- 2001–4000
- 4000

◀ This map shows the external agricultural virtual water footprint of the United Kingdom. Each arrow points to the country of origin, and the figures indicate the amount of "virtual" water imported per year as a result of purchasing food products, including cocoa, soybeans, coffee, livestock products, cotton, rice, and tea.

Home and Abroad

A country's water footprint is calculated by adding together the amount of water used from national water resources, such as groundwater sources and reservoirs, and adding it to the amount of water used from other countries. For example, the U.S. has an yearly average water footprint of 87,580 ft³ (2,480 m³) while China has an average footprint of 24,720 ft³ (700 m³). The global average water footprint is 43,790 ft³ (1,240 m³).

Stretched Resources

• The UK imports oranges and grapes from Spain, but in 2008 Spain had to import drinking water from France because it could not supply its population.

• A T-shirt made from cotton grown in Pakistan uses up 713 gallons (2,700 L) of water. The cotton was most likely to have been irrigated with water from the Indus River, which fell to its lowest-ever level in 2008.

"There's an important role for the public here. As a consumer you can ask businesses, including your local supermarkets, to tell you what they are doing to ensure good water management along their supply chains."

Stuart Orr, WWF 's UK water footprint expert

This irrigation rig is called a circular pivot or "king spin" system. The massive metal arm rotates around the crop delivering more or less water, depending on the weather conditions. ▼

Campaign: Big Business and Water

The World Wildlife Fund (WWF) is working with the retailer Marks & Spencer in a bid to estimate the size of the company's virtual water footprint for all of its food and clothing ranges. Marks & Spencer are tracing the production footsteps of five of its most popular products—strawberries, tomatoes, lettuce, potatoes, and roses—in an effort to identify suppliers with the least-impactful water usage.

"We are already in discussion with WWF about our decisions about where to grow crops in the future."

David Gregory, Technical Director, Marks & Spencer

Too Much Water: Flood

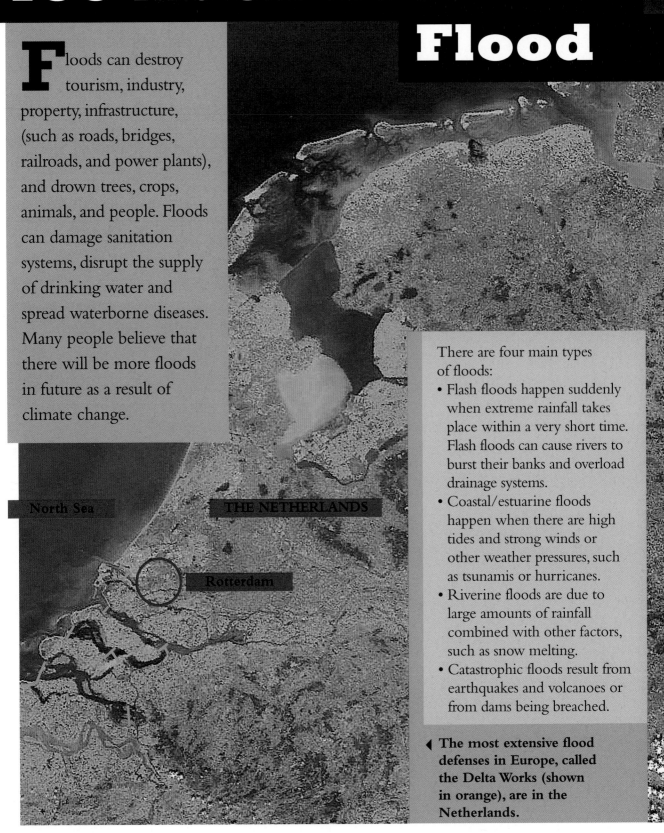

Floods can destroy tourism, industry, property, infrastructure, (such as roads, bridges, railroads, and power plants), and drown trees, crops, animals, and people. Floods can damage sanitation systems, disrupt the supply of drinking water and spread waterborne diseases. Many people believe that there will be more floods in future as a result of climate change.

North Sea

THE NETHERLANDS

Rotterdam

There are four main types of floods:
- Flash floods happen suddenly when extreme rainfall takes place within a very short time. Flash floods can cause rivers to burst their banks and overload drainage systems.
- Coastal/estuarine floods happen when there are high tides and strong winds or other weather pressures, such as tsunamis or hurricanes.
- Riverine floods are due to large amounts of rainfall combined with other factors, such as snow melting.
- Catastrophic floods result from earthquakes and volcanoes or from dams being breached.

◄ **The most extensive flood defenses in Europe, called the Delta Works (shown in orange), are in the Netherlands.**

"We can never eliminate the risk of flooding, particularly as climate change takes hold, but all of us . . . must take flood risk seriously and be as prepared as we can be to deal with it."

Hilary Benn, Environment Secretary, 2008

Case Study: Summer 2007 in Britain

In May, June, and July of 2007, England and Wales experienced 16.3 inches (414.1 mm) of rainfall—more than at any time since records began in 1766. Water levels were very high by the middle of June when, on June 24–25, a downpour threw northeast and central England into chaos. A month later, flash floods took hold of southeast, central, and northeast England. Britain's Environment Agency reported that 56,000 homes and businesses were flooded and 13 people killed. The floods cost the UK economy $4.9 billion.

Britain has implemented new technology and put plans in place to deal with the threat of future floods:

- Laser mapping of England and Wales is underway—this will identify all areas at risk of flooding.
- $266 million was spent in 2007 on building new flood defenses.
- CCTV has been installed on high-risk waterways so that blockages can be spotted and dealt with immediately.
- There is now 24-hour-a-day monitoring of rainfall, river levels, and coastal conditions.

Debate: Destroy Homes and Save Lives?

In 1993 floods devastated the Midwest United States causing $15 billion of damage, wrecking 50,000 homes, and claiming the lives of 50 people. After the floods, federal and state governments bought 25,000 properties that were liable to flood again and demolished them. This area was then made into wetlands. When the floods returned in 1995, the wetlands soaked up the water like a sponge, reducing the damage to remaining homes, farms, and fields.

Do you think governments of low-lying countries should buy up flood-prone areas and use them as barriers?

Catcliffe, in south Yorkshire, UK, was one of the worst-hit towns in 2007. It was evacuated because a nearby dam was under threat of collapse from floodwaters. ▼

▲ Laser mapping can show the surface of the Earth in three dimensions. A Lidar unit, fixed underneath an aircraft, scans the ground below 100,000 times a second. It can be used to show ground that is liable to flooding, and help plan flood evacuations.

Droughts threaten the quality of remaining water supplies for both people and wildlife. Water levels at reservoirs, such as this one, often become low during the summer.
▼

Not Enough Water: Drought

The world has always suffered from droughts—it is a natural part of the planet's weather patterns and seasons. But climate change is making weather patterns and the seasons less and less predictable, and droughts are becoming more frequent and more severe.

What Is Drought?

A drought is a lack of rain, usually for an extended period of time. Drought means different things to different people. If you're a farmer, then a drought means there isn't enough water to feed the crops you grow or the animals you tend. If you are a hydrologist, then a drought can be a time when there are very low levels of groundwater. Meteorologists measure a drought by looking at the amount of rainfall there is at any one time, compared with existing records.

Where You Are

Drought means different things depending on where you are in the world. Deserts are dry and hot, and have very little rainfall throughout the year. A drought in a desert can last for several years. Tropical regions have an almost constant supply of rain, so a drought in the tropics can be six days without rain.

What You Need

Drought also depends on what people need. There may be a serious and long-lasting drought in a desert, but if no one lives there, no crops are grown there, and few animals inhabit the area, then does the drought have a big effect? The consequences of reduced rainfall in a heavily populated area that also has high concentrations of farms and livestock can be devastating. Soon, people don't have enough water to drink, wash, and cook. Crops fail and animals die.

> "Seasonal rains have been poor or have failed in many parts of Ethiopia, with dramatic effects on harvests in crop-producing areas."

Elisabeth Byrs, spokeswoman for the United Nations Office for the Coordination of Humanitarian Affairs, June 2008

Facts

- The World Meteorological Organization (WMO) monitors droughts worldwide and tries to warn governments before droughts take hold. If farmers are given enough time, they can plant crops that need less water.
- In Thailand, in 2005, planes flew above the clouds over 1,000 times in a month spraying salt, dry ice, and silver iodine into them. This is called cloud seeding—it forces water vapor to mix and fall as rain.

- It is estimated that drought costs the United States $6-8 billion every year due to its impact on areas such as agriculture, forestry, and tourism. The U.S. National Drought Mitigation Center has been established to help states formulate drought action plans.

Campaign: Preparing for Drought

The African Drought Risk & Development Network has been developed by the UN Development Programme Drylands Development Center and the International Strategy for Disaster Reduction Africa. The network informs people how to plan for drought and reduce its impact via meetings, consultations, conferences, and web-based information and discussion forums. Practical advice, including waterfall predictions and rain reports, is given to environmental and agriculture planners so that long-term issues can be tackled. News sources are briefed on drought issues so that broadcasts can be made.

Preparing the sprays on a cloud-seeding plane. Cloud seeding can be unreliable as results depend on many factors, such as humidity and the type of clouds being sprayed. ▼

Case Study: The World's Driest Inhabited Continent

In 2003, a drought began in many parts of Australia, including South Australia, New South Wales, and the Murray-Darling Basin.

Thanks to recent rainfall, some areas, such as New South Wales, have since come out of the drought, but others, such as Central Victoria, are still struggling with low water reserves. The Murray-Darling Basin, which is a bit smaller than the state of Alaska and supplies Australia with 85 percent of the water it needs for irrigation, is still affected and is in danger of ecological collapse.

The effects of the Australian drought have been felt in the rest of the world. The grain harvest has been reduced, driving up prices of wheat. Australia's dairy industry exports to 130 countries, but exports have been cut because dairy cattle have been affected by the drought. This has driven up the price of milk in other countries.

The drought in Australia has changed the way people think about water. States have been forced to produce drought-response plans that make farmers, industry, and individuals use this precious resource sparingly.

Measures include:
- generous government rebates for homeowners who plumb in rainwater tanks, install efficient showerheads, and buy systems for reusing household water;
- water efficiency in industry—the vegetable industry is now twice as efficient in its use of water as it was a decade ago;
- investments in desalination plants. In Perth, a new desalination plant opened in 2006, making Western Australia the first state in Australia to use desalination as a primary water source. The Perth plant supplies 17 percent of the city's water needs.

▲ A dry bank on the Murray River. Australia depends on the Murray-Darling Basin for 40 percent of its agricultural produce.

"It is a grim situation, and there is no point in pretending to Australia otherwise. We must all hope and pray there is rain."

John Howard, Prime Minister of Australia (1996–2007), speaking in 2007

▲ The desalination plant at Kwinana, Perth supplies 1.5 million people with drinkable water.

Aquifer Greed and the Rainwater Revolution

People all over the world rely on aquifers to feed their crops and quench their thirst. China, India, and the U.S. are the world's main grain producers—and all of these countries are over-extracting water from their aquifers to irrigate their land.

Types of Aquifers

There are different types of aquifers. Shallow aquifers can be found near the surface of the ground and consist of rocks, gravel, sand, or clay that hold water in the same way as a sponge. These aquifers can be accessed with wells dug by hand or water can be extracted via pumps. A lot of these aquifers can be replenished by rainwater.

Deep, or fossil, aquifers lie thousands of feet underground and contain water that has filtered down into confined spaces within rocks over tens of thousands of years. These aquifers are more likely to be non-replenishable. When this water runs out, farming could become extremely difficult.

▲ These fertile circles of crops in Saudi Arabia are irrigated by water extracted from a fossil aquifer over half a mile (1 km) under the sands of the desert. It has cost $40 billion to extract this ancient water and most of it evaporates as soon as it meets the heat of the Sun.

> "The overuse of water in Asia's underground aquifers will spell disaster for millions of the region's poor people who depend on it."
>
> Tushaar Shah, Director of the International Water Management Institute groundwater research station, Gujarat, India

Need or Greed?

In India it is estimated that 21 million farmers extract water from underground water sources, causing the water table to drop every year. This water is being taken at an estimated rate of 60 million cubic miles (250 million km^3) a year—but rain can only replace about 36 million cubic miles (150 million km^3) of this water every year. It is thought that a quarter of India's farmers are taking underground water that cannot be replaced. In the bearly 1900s, wells in rural areas were typically 33 feet (10 m) deep. Now half of the hand-dug wells of India are dry and new wells are being sunk to a depth of 1,312 feet (400 m)—and they are still running dry.

> "Yes, I'm worried that the water will disappear. But what can I do? I have to live, and if I don't pump it up, my neighbors will."
>
> Jitbhai Chowdhury, dairy farmer, Gujarat, India

▲ In India millions of farmers use cheap Japanese-made pumps to take water out of aquifers. This water grows about two-thirds of India's crops every year, ensuring that millions of people do not starve.

▲ Many countries have had water reservoirs for centuries. This baoli, or step well, dates from ca. 900 and is in Ram Kund, Mandu, India. New technology could help people to collect and use rainwater in a similar way.

One of the ways that aquifers can be protected is to reduce or stop the extraction of water from them. This can happen when whole communities get their water from somewhere else. The most obvious place to get water is the sky because water on Earth starts with rain. Rain falls from the sky to replenish rivers, lakes, ponds, and groundwater. It is cheaper and far more efficient to collect rainwater than it is to dig and pump wells, build dams, or lay thousands of miles of water pipes.

Harvesting Rainwater

In many countries, people have harvested or collected water since the earliest times. In Britain, a water barrel sitting in a garden collecting rain is the most basic form of rainwater harvesting. In some parts of China, people divert rainwater from their roofs into purpose-built cellars in a tradition that stretches back 2,000 years.

Tradition and the Future

Now governments and non-governmental organizations (NGOs) all over the world—from Brazil to India—are recognizing the value of rainwater harvesting and are working to restore and promote traditional rainwater collection practices. They are also creating new strategies for rainwater harvesting.

Case Study: *Jal Swaraj*—Water Self-Reliance in India

The Center for Science and Environment (CSE), an NGO based in New Delhi, educates people about traditional rainwater harvesting techniques —everything from rooftop collection systems in cities, to low mud walls around fields in rural areas that direct rain back into village wells and replenish groundwater. This is called *Jal Swaraj*—water self-reliance—and it is putting control of water as a resource back into the hands of individuals and communities.

CSE Campaign Facts

- Rain centers have been established by the CSE in cities throughout India. Rain centers show permanent exhibitions about water conservation, rainwater harvesting, and water education in an attempt to spread "water literacy" within India's urban communities.

- *Jal Yodhas*, or water warriors, are individuals who are setting good examples of water use within communities and pioneering rainwater harvesting.

- It is estimated that 20,000 villages in India are now harvesting rain.

"The Real Green Revolution is about rainwater harvesting. Let us catch water where it falls. Let it transform human lives. Let it change social existence. If this happens, the world will be transformed."

Anil Agarwal, Founder-Director of the Center for Science and Environment (CSE), New Delhi, India

Bad Pollution

Polluted water is not clean enough to drink, to irrigate crops, to feed animals, or to protect and support diverse arrays of plant and animal life. Some rivers around the world are getting cleaner, but many are biologically dead. Polluted water has a direct effect on human sanitation. Poor sanitation leads to 2.2 million child deaths annually around the world.

Many Pollutants

Water can be polluted by many of the things that humans do. Here are just a few causes of water pollution:

- Farmers grow more crops if they use fertilizer, but the chemicals in fertilizers "run off" the land into watercourses and find their way into drinking water
- Factories produce waste that is sometimes dumped into rivers, without first being treated to make it safe
- Human and animal waste is often dumped into rivers
- Smoke from factories contains chemicals that are released into the atmosphere and can come back to Earth as acid rain. The chemicals can enter the water supply through aquifers and rivers—where they become part of the water supply.

"An estimated 42,000 people die every week from diseases related to low water quality and an absence of adequate sanitation. This situation is unacceptable."

Ban Ki-Moon, United Nations Secretary-General, 2008

Campaign: Pottery Power

Potters for Peace is an American organization dedicated to reducing the disease and death caused by polluted water. In Latin America, Africa, and Asia, Potters for Peace (see image below, left) teach local potters how to make ceramic water filters that look like large flower pots. The pots are made of clay mixed with sawdust or ground rice husks. The sawdust/rice husks burn off while the pot undergoes firing, leaving behind tiny holes. The pots are then painted with a silver solution that kills bacteria. When the pots are placed inside a water container the holes block waterborne bacteria and let clean water seep through. Tests have shown that this simple and cheap pot reduces 99.88 percent of the bacteria that cause diarrhea—a major contributor to child deaths. About 300,000 filters have been made and are currently used by 1.5 million people.

"You put dirty water in—gray water that many communities still drink—and it comes out crystal clear."

Ron Rivera (1948–2008), Coordinator of the Ceramic Water Filter Program, Potters for Peace

▲ More than a billion people still do not have access to clean drinking water.

It has taken 25 years to remove 80 percent of the chemicals that were killing Barton Broad. ▼

Case Study:
Restoring The Norfolk Broads in England

The Norfolk Broads are a collection of seven rivers and 63 lakes (known as "broads") in Norfolk and Suffolk, and form the UK's biggest protected wetland. Barton Broad became seriously polluted as a result of modern farming and the presence of two sewage treatment plants. This pollution created thick, black mud that killed plants and fish. In the 1990s, mud from Barton Broad was pumped out as part of a wetland restoration project. In the end about 160 Olympic-size swimming pools of mud were pumped out. With the sewage treatment plants cleaned up too, clean water flowed back into the Broad. A mud pump then continued to clean the water for four years. Tourists have been able to enjoy Barton Broad more since the cleanup—a long suspended walkway has been put in place so that visitors can experience the Broad without further damage to its ecosystem.

Good Pollution?

In less developed countries, village after village may have to share one stream and this water will be used for everything—from drinking, cooking, and washing to feeding animals and watering crops. In situations such as this, it is very difficult for people to protect themselves from diseases introduced via wild animals drinking, bathing, or dying in the same water, or from the pollution created by villages, towns, or industries located upstream.

Is Water Pollution Sometimes a Good Thing?

Agriculture is the biggest consumer of water in the world. Many farmers in less developed countries do not have access to clean water to irrigate their land—about 49 million acres (20 million hectares) of farming land is irrigated with water rife with raw sewage. In Pakistan, farming land near a sewage source is worth more than land near a clean water supply. The sewage-water land has the advantage of an uninterrupted irrigation supply that fertilizes the soil at the same time. The farmers are prone to skin diseases and waterborne illnesses, but they grow a lot of food and make more money than the farmers who only use freshwater.

"We need to recognize that sewage is a valuable resource that grows huge amounts of food. So instead we should help the millions of farmers involved do it better."

Chris Scott, International Water Management Institute (IWMI)

◀ An estimated 200 million farmers around the world use polluted water from a source like this to irrigate their crops. Some of these farmers are urban, based in slums in major cities, and cultivate tiny patches of food that feed many people.

Moving Forward with Dirty Water

Some countries have recognized that polluted water can be an essential part of their national water management policy. Mexico, Kuwait, Saudi Arabia, Oman, Egypt, Tunisia, Jordan, and Israel have all started to treat sewage to a standard that can be used for irrigation—thereby protecting stocks of highly valuable freshwater for drinking. Some scientists think that treated polluted water is actually better than freshwater for farming because it contains nitrogen and phosphorus—substances that contribute to higher crop yields. Other scientists are concerned about the potential health effects of irrigating with wastewater. No one actually knows what the long-term health implications of this practice will be.

▲ In Israel, 80 percent of the country's treated wastewater is used for irrigation.

Debate: Is Dirty Water better than No Water?

Many farmers in less developed countries store wastewater in large tanks to let the sediment fall to the bottom, then they skim the best water off the top. Other farmers take water directly from sewers in order to grow food that they would not otherwise be able to afford.

These farmers do not have a choice; freshwater is not available for irrigation. Given the potential health risks, many of which have not been fully examined, should these farmers be forced to stop using dirty water? Or should more be done to control dirty water quality?

In Tunisia, 62 wastewater plants have been established to treat wastewater for agriculture. Wastewater should not be used for water-intensive crops, such as lettuce, that are not cooked before being eaten. ▼

Water Supply

To get water, most people in developed countries just turn on a tap. But many people in less developed countries do not have a tap to turn on. How we obtain water influences how we use, how much it costs us, and how healthy we are.

Water Here

Developed nations divert rivers, create reservoirs, and build pipelines that carry water huge distances. Rich countries invest in water treatment plants and new technologies such as desalination, and the quality of drinking water is monitored at national government level. The majority of people in developed countries pay for water as part of their utility bills and, as a percentage of income, water is cheap.

Many people in rural areas of less developed countries still have to carry water from wells or rivers. ▼

▲ It is thought that 33–50 percent of the water going into water mains worldwide is lost through waste (above) or leaks (right). ▶

Water There

Although many less developed nations have water infrastructures, or are in the process of putting them in place, sometimes investment is underfunded and the systems are poorly maintained. Some people in rural areas of less developed nations have to get water wherever they can—from rivers, lakes, and streams. People in villages also sink boreholes, or people, usually women and children, walk for miles to draw water from communal wells. In some parts of the world the urban poor have a piped water supply, but it is often unreliable and has little or no regulation, meaning that there is no guarantee of its purity. As a percentage of their income, it is also very expensive. Some people do not even have that, and are at the mercy of suppliers who bring in water using trucks. They sell the water at whatever the market rate is.

> "Halve, by 2015, the proportion of people without sustainable access to safe water and basic sanitation."
>
> United Nations Millennium Development Goal Number 7, Target 10

Water Resource or Water Supply?

When scientists talk about water resources, they are referring to all the water that is available for agriculture, industry, and domestic use. Water supply is a term that refers to treated water that is suitable for drinking. The gap between water resources and water supply tends to be smaller in poorer countries, where people do not differentiate between the two categories of water—often because for them it is the same "pool." The richer the country, the bigger the difference in the management of water resources and water supply.

Water Equity

One of the key issues in water sustainability is continuity and equity of supply—at the moment the richest people in the world pay relatively little for their water and have plenty of it; the poorest people in the world pay the most for water and cannot always get it; and those that cannot afford clean water drink dirty water or die of thirst.

Campaign: More Crop per Drop

Agriculture is the most water-intensive activity in the world. When water resources are low, supply is intermittent and crops fail and people starve. Even where there is ample water, it is sometimes distributed indiscriminately or does not reach the plants that need it. Farming communities, governments, and NGOs are being forced to come up with new ways of getting "more crop per drop" as a way of conserving water resources and easing pressure on supply.

- Microirrigation kits are an easy-to-use technology that cost as little as $1 for a kit that can irrigate 24 square yards (20 m^2) of soil. Instead of pouring water into the ground, drip irrigation feeds water to the crops at a steady rate, like a tap dripping. Farmers using cheap drip kits can produce 40 percent more food using half the usual amount of water.

- In wealthy places, such as the U.S., expensive, high-tech irrigation systems that include pressure gauges, flow meters, and instruments sensitive to soil moisture, deliver water to crops so efficiently that water usage in these places has dropped by a third.

Case Study: Singapore and the Four National Taps Strategy

Singapore is an island nation in southeast Asia with a population of 4.5 million people crammed into an area only slightly larger than New York City.

The "Two Taps"

Singapore has always relied on rainwater (50 percent) and imports of water from Malaysia (50 percent). The Singapore government has referred to these water sources as the "two national taps."

In 2002, the government decided to take action to reduce the country's reliance on imported water and to diversify their water supply. This was called the Four National Taps strategy. The "four taps" are:

- tap 1 – rainfall
- tap 2 – imported water
- tap 3 – reclaimed water
- tap 4 – desalination.

Tap 3: Reclaimed Water

Starting in 2003, 2 million gallons (7 million L) of water reclaimed from sewers was put back into Singapore's water network. Today this is used for industry, but in the future it will be used in people's homes. This reclaimed water represents only 1 percent of Singapore's daily water consumption, but the volume of reclaimed water will rise to 2.5 percent by 2011.

Tap 4: Desalination

Desalination is a process that makes seawater drinkable. In 2005, the Tuas desalination plant in Singapore was opened. Tuas is one of the most energy-efficient desalination plants in the world and produces the cheapest desalinated seawater on Earth. It now supplies 10 percent of Singapore's water. The plant cost $200 million and the water price varies according to fuel costs.

▲ Part of the desalination plant in Singapore that opened in 2005. It is the largest in Asia.

▲ A student studying a GIS map. These interactive maps can help us to understand how water and sanitation are connected, and which areas are in most need of investment and support.

Water Mapping

One of the problems with water supply in a developing country is figuring out who has access to water and sanitation in rural areas. Water mapping can fill in these information gaps.

Various NGOs, such as WaterAid, are conducting valuable work creating water maps in places such as Malawi, Tanzania, Nepal, Pakistan, and West Africa. Teams of researchers travel out into the country—in cars, on foot, on bicycles—with hand-held GPS devices and notebooks to locate water points, such as wells, pumps, and boreholes. This information is then matched up with population records to establish how many people utilize each water source.

Water maps detail the following kinds of information:

• How much water is available and its quality. Seasonal changes, such as droughts and floods, must also be taken into account

• Water uses—for washing, mining, brewing, farming, cooking, drinking etc.

• Access to water and sanitation —establishing which people need water and sanitation and who has oversupply

All this up-to-date knowledge is put into a database where it can be viewed in the form of a digital map. Water mapping can pinpoint inequalities of water services and can be used to lobby governments to redistribute water supplies.

Watersheds

Almost every person on Earth lives near a watershed. Any area of land where water drains to a collection point, such as an aquifer, estuary, river, stream, lake, or the ocean, is a watershed. Water also filters through the ground to enter a watershed.

Watershed management is a complex task, especially as human development, such as expanding urban areas, continues to affect them. ▼

Watershed Protection

Without healthy and protected watersheds, river, lake, and ocean habitats die. We need to sustain watersheds in order to make water itself sustainable.

To protect the quality of water in a river, we need to look after the land in the river's watershed —because the quality of the water flowing into the river affects the quality of the water that we take out to use in agriculture and to drink. Water quality also affects wildlife habitats.

Watershed Destruction

Over the centuries we have interfered with watersheds in every way possible. As land use has changed we have:

- Built up areas including cities, leading to physical interference with the watershed, increased pollutants in the water cycle, and over-extraction of water for agriculture, drinking water, and domestic use
- Cut down trees, leading to soil erosion that allows rainwater to "run off" the land into watercourses, carrying soil with it as a pollutant
- Dammed rivers, changing the course of rivers and destroying wildlife habitats.

Case Study:
The World's Biggest Watershed Restoration Project

The Everglades in southern Florida is a wetland area of global importance.

People began building canals to divert water from the Everglades in the 1880s. This encouraged rapid urban and farming development. By 1947, 1,429 miles (2,300 km) of canals had been built and 50 percent of the Everglades were lost. The South Florida area grew rapidly.

Some effects of over-extracting water from the Everglades watershed:

- Newly-created fields covered with fertilizer leached phosphorus into the soil, either killing or changing the plant life of the area
- A drop in the quality of water, less water storage capacity, and water shortages
- A reduction in wading bird numbers of 85 percent (over 50 years)

Save it or Lose it

In 1995, an investigation into the sustainability of the South Florida metropolitan area concluded that its urban areas were no longer sustainable, and that if the South Florida ecosystem was not salvaged, then the local tourism industry would lose 12,000 jobs and an annual income of $200 million. Commercial fishing would also suffer, losing over $50 million a year.

The Plan

In 2000, the Comprehensive Everglades Restoration Plan (CERP) was established. CERP restores as much of the Everglades as possible and is the biggest and most expensive environmental rescue plan in history. The plan covers an area of 10,811 mi^2 (28,000 km^2) and crosses 16 counties.

CERP Facts

- The plan consists of 50 projects.
- It will take 30 years to implement.
- The estimated cost is currently $10.5 billion.

How CERP Works

- Fresh, currently unused, water that travels to the ocean is being caught and stored in aquifers, reservoirs, and abandoned quarries. It is then sent to areas that need to be environmentally

▲ Between 1947 and 1995 the Everglades were tamed, channeled, and drained to suit the needs of urban development.

Unspoiled watersheds can be beautiful places, home to biodiverse populations of plants and animals. ▼

restored. Any water that is left over goes to urban areas and farms, thereby taking pressure off existing water extraction of the Everglades.

- Stormwater treatment areas are being created, with the goal of filtering mercury from the water that falls into the Everglades from rainwater polluted by the burning of fossil fuels from local power plants.
- Reuse of wastewater in urban areas.
- Dismantling of canals.

CERP News Update

In June 2008, the State of Florida bought the company U.S. Sugar for $1.7 billion. The company will run for another six years and then all the employees will be let go and its factories, warehouses, and railroad lines will be demolished. All of the company's land will be restored to a natural state.

Still a Long Way to Go

The CERP has decades to run before the wetlands are restored and a sustainable water supply is established. There are still significant problems with mercury contamination, threats to bird populations, and canals discharge over 1.8 billion gallons (7 billion L) of water a day into the ocean—diverting it from the wetlands where it should be. But a lot of progress has been made: the Kissimmee River is under restoration, water flow into the Everglades National Park has been improved, and in the northern Everglades, treatment marshes have been established to improve water quality.

" There are no other Everglades in the world."
Marjory Stoneman Douglas, *The Everglades: River of Grass*, 1947

Rivers and Dams

A river is a body of running water that follows a distinct course and is usually comprised of freshwater. Rivers run into other rivers, into lakes, and into oceans. Rivers receive their water from streams, springs, rain, melting snow, or glaciers, and excess water from lakes and other rivers.

▶ Regional distribution of rivers over 620 miles (1,000 km) long and percentage of rivers remaining free-flowing.

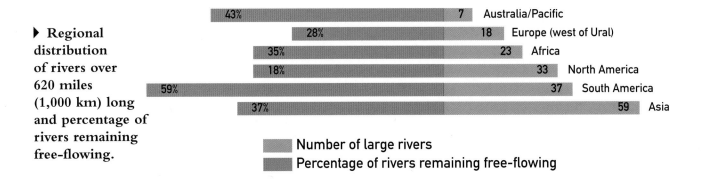

43%	7	Australia/Pacific
28%	18	Europe (west of Ural)
35%	23	Africa
18%	33	North America
59%	37	South America
37%	59	Asia

■ Number of large rivers
■ Percentage of rivers remaining free-flowing

What Rivers Do for Us

Rivers have always been our main source of drinking water and water for agriculture. Rivers provide us with drainage, transportation, food, energy (through hydroelectric power), and opportunities for recreation. Human habitation began alongside rivers and most capital cities are on the banks of a great waterway.

From Pure to Polluted

The place where a river begins, called the source, is where the purest water is usually found. As the river grows in volume and travels along its course, it picks up natural pollutants from the soil, such as silt and minerals, and artificial pollutants such as human waste, factory by-products, and agricultural runoff.

The only fishing that people living along the banks of the Citarum River in Indonesia do is for garbage that can be re-used or sold for a few dollars a week. Nine million people from the nearby city of Jakarta dump their untreated sewage into the Citarum, as well as over 500 factories. Water from this river is used for washing, irrigation and, for the poorest, as drinking water. ▼

From Free-Running to Contained

The power of rivers has also attracted development. The courses of rivers have been changed by dams and weirs to generate hydroelectricity, and canals built to provide transport links. Dams—some of the biggest structures ever made—have had a huge physical impact on rivers, flood plains, and the surrounding area.

Dams, such as this one on the Danube at Vienna, have altered the course and biology of an estimated 60 percent of the biggest river systems on the planet.

"Problems may be magnified as more large dams are added to a river system, resulting in an increased and cumulative loss of natural resources, habitat quality, environmental sustainability and ecosystem integrity."

World Commission on Dams report, 2000

Facts about Rivers

- The longest river is the Nile River at 4,145 miles (6,670 km).
- The only continent without any rivers is Antarctica.
- The river with the biggest annual volume of water is the Amazon—it holds 1,439 cubic miles (6,000 km^3) of water. The annual flow of the Nile, by comparison, is 12 cubic miles (50 km^3) of water.

Superdams

In 1935, the completion of the Hoover Dam in Nevada heralded the age of the "superdam." The Hoover is more than 725 feet (221 meters) high and is larger than the Great Pyramid in Egypt. The biggest dam project in the world at the moment is the Three Gorges Dam—it crosses the Yangtze River in China and is over five times larger than the Hoover Dam. The Three Gorges Dam is scheduled for completion in 2011.

Campaign: Taking Care of the Danube River

The Danube River runs through 17 countries in Europe, bringing together the 80 million people who live along its banks. Over the years, the river has become polluted, flood plains have been built upon, and nearby forests have been cut down. In the year 2000, the European Union brought in the EU Water Framework Directive. The directive adopts a Europe-wide approach to the care of the Danube by consulting environmentalists, residents, and industry and agriculture experts, with the aim of improving water quality by 2015. The management of the river is an enormous task, as more than four-fifths of the Danube is flood-protected and 700 dams and spillways have been built along its main waterways.

Dismantling Dams

During the second half of the twentieth century, institutions such as the World Bank financed dam-building programs all over the world, particularly in less developed countries. Dams were seen as the answer to the long-term management of water in water-scarce areas—even by many environmentalists. But recently, doubts have been cast on the sustainability of dam projects.

- Is the loss of unique species of river birds, crocodiles, dolphins, and fish worth it?
- Can the loss of wetlands and fisheries be justified to future generations?
- Do the people who are removed from their homes in order to construct the dams benefit from the electricity that they generate?
- Are these people ever compensated for the livelihoods they lose once their homes and fields are flooded?
- Do dams distribute enough water to enough people to justify their enormous cost?

▲ In the U.S. some dams are now being destroyed. Between 1999 and 2006, 654 dams were dismantled in the U.S.

Debate: The Three Gorges Dam

Do you think that the Three Gorges Dam should have been built?

Pros

The Three Gorges Dam will:

- Provide cheap electricity for thousands of Chinese homes
- Reduce greenhouse gases by reducing China's dependence on coal-based power stations
- Increase the quality of wastewater being put into the Three Gorges reservoir thanks to new water treatment plants (currently 65 percent of wastewater is treated)
- Control seasonal flooding
- Protect against drought
- Increase the productivity of agricultural land via improved irrigation.

Cons

The Three Gorges Dam has:

- Uprooted 1.24 million people from their homes
- Destroyed important architecture, archaeological sites, natural habitats and disrupted communities
- Cost $30 billion
- Put species such as the Siberian Crane and the Yangtze river dolphin (the Baiji) under threat
- Increased pollution of the Yangtze River in the long term
- Increased deforestation and soil erosion along the banks of the Yangtze River.

▲ The Three Gorges Dam has radically altered the landscape of this important tourist area. Supporters of the dam say that tourists will be just as interested in viewing the new dam as they were in seeing the old landscape, so tourism will be unaffected.

Facts About Dams

- There are an estimated 50,000 dams in the world.
- About 1,500 dams are currently under construction worldwide.
- About a fifth of the world's electricity is generated by hydroelectric dams.
- The 20 largest rivers in the world all have dams on them.
- It is estimated that 80 million rural people have been removed from their homes in order to create dams.

"... the direct adverse impacts of dams have fallen disproportionately on rural dwellers, subsistence farmers, indigenous peoples, ethnic minorities, and women."

World Commission on Dams report, 2000

The Future

If anything is sustainable, it is water. The water cycle is constantly engaged in the process of giving us our water back—the problem is making sure that the water is where we need it to be when it needs to be there. The challenge lies in causing as little damage as possible to the environment of the world as we extract the water that we need to live.

Possible Solutions

Water needs to be managed as a worldwide resource, on a truly global scale. Here are just some of the things that need to happen around the world for water to become more sustainable and for the distribution of water to become fairer.

- There needs to be effective cooperation between nations that share rivers and aquifers.
- Water needs to be used as efficiently as possible by industry, agriculture, and the general population.
- Agriculture needs to reduce its water usage by improving irrigation techniques, using rainwater harvesting, and growing crops that need less water.
- Research into alternative sources of energy needs to be conducted with a view to taking some of the pressure for electricity generation off large dams.
- Watershed conservation needs to be integrated into all levels of rural and urban planning.

"The key to avoiding catastrophic water shortages is bringing people out of poverty."

Professor Tony Allan, King's College, London

▲ These students from the African Medical and Research Foundation (AMREF) are digging a well in a village where people usually have to travel significant distances to obtain water.

Debate: Which Way to Sustainability?

There is currently a battle going on between high-tech water management methods, such as big dams, expensive desalination plants, and engineering projects that divert rivers, and cheaper approaches in less developed countries. These approaches include the use of intermediate technologies, such as rainwater harvesting, hand-sunk, properly-monitored wells, and composting latrines instead of flushing toilets. Combined with education, the intermediate technologies are affordable and achievable, if governments and populations want them.

Campaign: Trading Virtual Water

Leading academics have called upon the World Trade Organization (WTO) to set up a virtual-water trading council. Supporters argue that effective trading of virtual water would encourage countries with pressured water resources to import products that need a lot of water to produce, thereby safeguarding their own water reserves for essential uses, such as drinking water.

"The main aim of the virtual-water trading council would be to ensure that the water replaced when food, electricity or industrial goods are imported is used to achieve sanitation outcomes in the importing country. Also that the exporting country does not endanger the health of its citizens by exporting."

Jennifer McKay, Director of the Centre for Comparative Water Policies and Laws, University of South Australia

Glossary

aquifer: a formation in the ground that can hold water like a sponge. Water can be extracted from an aquifer.

dam: a barrier placed across a body of water to catch or hold water in one place.

desalination: the removal of salt and/or minerals from water so that it can be consumed by human beings. Desalination of water on a large scale is very expensive and uses a lot of energy.

freshwater: natural water that has a low level of salts and is suitable for drinking.

GIS: a Geographic Information System (GIS) converts information from a database into map form so that it can be more easily interpreted and understood.

GPS: a Global Positioning System (GPS) can tell you exactly where something is located on Earth by timing the signals sent by GPS satellites in space.

groundwater: any water that sits below the surface of the Earth embedded in the water table.

hydroelectric power: the name given to electricity generated by falling water, usually dammed water. Hydroelectricity is currently the world's main source of renewable energy (63 percent).

hydrologist: someone who studies water.

initiative: a long-term plan with clear aims, often backed by government support.

intermediate technology: technology that is easy to use and affordable to individuals in developing nations.

meteorologist: someone who studies the science of the atmosphere.

NGO (Non-Governmental Organization): an organization that is not linked to or part of a government, often run as a charity.

runoff: rain that flows as a stream or as part of a river.

saltwater: water that has a high salt content. Human beings cannot drink saltwater.

sustainable: capable of being maintained, especially in an environmentally sound manner.

virtual water: the amount of freshwater that was used to produce things such as clothing and food.

wastewater: any water that has waste in it, such as animal, human, or industrial waste.

water cycle: the stages water goes through from its fall to Earth as rain, its passage into the water table, then its rise via evaporation back into the air to form clouds.

water footprint: the amount of water an individual, household or organization uses on a daily basis.

watershed: a piece of land where excess water lies or falls to.

water table: the name given to the point at which the soil below the surface of the ground is saturated with water.

weir: a dam in a stream or river to raise the water level or divert its flow

wetlands: any area of land whose soil is saturated with water, such as a swamp or a bog. Wetlands often sit between the land and areas of water and are places that support a huge variety of animal and plant life.

Web Sites

African Drought Risk & Development Network
www.droughtnet.org
An organization that educates people on how to plan for a drought.

Center for Science and Environment (CSE)
www.rainwaterharvesting.org
For a full explanation of the Jal Swaraj (water self-reliance) campaign as well as practical information on rainwater harvesting, raincenters, newsletters and events, awards, and publications.

Comprehensive Everglades Restoration Plan (CERP)
www.evergladesplan.org
The official site of the Everglades Restoration Plan.

H20 Conserve
www.H2Oconserve.org
Calculate how much water your household uses every day with this online calculator.

International Rivers (IR)
www.internationalrivers.org
For current information on the state of rivers and news of the communities that depend upon rivers, all over the world. Lots of up-to-date information on the decommissioning of dams. Slideshows and bulletins.

International Water Management Institute (IWMI)
www.iwmi.cgiar.org
Learn all about water management issues as they relate to agriculture, cities, people, and the environment.

Potters for Peace
www.pottersforpeace.org
All about the work of this NGO and how to help.

Practical Action
www.itdg.org
For information on a wide range of intermediate technologies. Practical Action is an NGO that promotes the use of affordable new technologies to assist water supply and sanitation projects (among others) in developing countries.

UNESCO
www.unesco.org/water
A portal to web links associated with the subject of water. Click on Water Links and then select a theme, a type of organization, or a geographical area.

United Nations: Water for Life
www.un.org/waterforlifedecade
The official web site of the United Nations Water for Life Decade (2005-2015). You can view a number of short films on the subject of water, including a video message from former UN Secretary-General Kofi Annan called "Water is essential for life." There is also reference material on freshwater and a calendar of events.

WaterAid
www.wateraid.org
This NGO works in 17 countries to help people's access to water and sanitation. Read about its projects all over the world.

Index